DIRT BIKE CRAZY

SUZUKI DIRT BIKES

By R. L. Van

Kaleidoscope
Minneapolis, MN

The Quest for Discovery Never Ends

This edition is co-published by agreement between Kaleidoscope and World Book, Inc.

Kaleidoscope Publishing, Inc.
6012 Blue Circle Drive
Minnetonka, MN 55343 U.S.A.

World Book, Inc.
180 North LaSalle St., Suite 900
Chicago IL 60601 U.S.A.

Kaleidoscope ISBNs
978-1-64519-094-3 (library bound)
978-1-64494-155-3 (paperback)
978-1-64519-198-8 (ebook)

World Book ISBN
978-0-7166-4367-8 (library bound)

Library of Congress Control Number
2019939020

Printed in the United States of America.

FIND ME IF YOU CAN!

Bigfoot lurks within one of the images in this book. It's up to you to find him!

TABLE OF CONTENTS

CHAPTER 1

Camp Carmichael

Mai zips up her jacket. She climbs onto the seat of her dirt bike. It's a Suzuki RM85. The wind stirs up dirt from the **motocross** track. Mai pulls on her goggles. She tightens her helmet strap. Today is the regional championship. Riders from all over the northeast United States are competing. She wants to do well. She wants to go to Camp Carmichael.

Many young riders like Mai choose to ride to victory on Suzuki dirt bikes.

In addition to his motocross success, Ricky Carmichael also raced for NASCAR.

Suzuki riders have a special opportunity. Riders win points at races during the year. The ones with the most points go to Camp Carmichael. Mai is a big fan of Ricky Carmichael. He had two perfect motocross seasons. He's the only rider to do this. He won the 2005 **supercross** title. It was on a Suzuki RM250. Carmichael runs a racing school now. He has a camp just for Suzuki riders. Mai has her eyes on the prize. People call Carmichael the "GOAT." It's short for "Greatest of All Time." Mai wants to learn from the GOAT.

FUN FACT

Ricky Carmichael's camps are held on his farm. He calls it the Goat Farm.

PARTS OF A SUZUKI RM-Z250

Mai lines up at the starting gate. Her RM85's fender is yellow. The **fork** rises up from the front wheel. A red *S*-shaped logo is on the side. The wind whips her ponytail. The gate drops. Mai speeds to the first corner. She doesn't get the **holeshot**. But that only makes her want to win more. She can learn new tricks if she makes it to Camp Carmichael.

Suzuki wants to help **amateurs** like Mai. Mai read about past winners. A couple girls in her racing class won in 2018. Mai is glad girls are making their mark on motocross. With her Suzuki bike, she can join them.

Suzuki pays for winning amateurs to attend Camp Carmichael.

CHAPTER 2

Victory Looming

It was 1909. Michio Suzuki lived in Japan. He was training in carpentry. He worked for a man who made **looms**. Soon, Suzuki founded Suzuki Loom Works. He invented a new type of loom. This made it easier to weave checked fabrics. He became very successful.

Suzuki had other dreams, too. He built a car. But then Japan entered World War II (1939–1945). He had to put his dream on hold.

Looms are used to weave fabric.

Then the war ended. In 1952, his son Shunzo had an idea. The wind in their town was very strong. Sometimes it was difficult to bike. What if bicycles had engines? Shunzo Suzuki built the Power Free. It was a motorized bicycle. The bike sold well. Michio Suzuki renamed his company. It became Suzuki Motor in 1954.

FUN FACT
Suzuki gave the first loom he built to his mom as a gift.

Gabe's dad loves dirt bikes. He especially loves old dirt bikes. His favorite is his 1976 Suzuki RM250A. Gabe's dad told him all about it. Suzuki had great pro racing bikes. They won the 1970 world championship. They won five more championships in the next six years.

Belgian rider Roger De Coster won five World Championships for Suzuki in the 1970s.

But the bike Suzuki sold to the public was different. It wasn't as good as the racing bike. Suzuki made a change. It put the RM250A on the market in 1976. This was more like the racing bike. It had great **suspension**. People thought it was the best bike in its class.

Gabe's favorite is the 1989 RM250. It doesn't have a blue motor like the RM250A. But it has a more rigid fork. And it looks much sleeker. The bike is lighter than earlier models. It turns really well. Turning corners is Suzuki's specialty. Gabe has a 2019 RM-Z125 now. But he's glad he knows so much about Suzuki's history. He loves learning about how the bikes have changed over time.

Suzuki's S logo was first used in 1958.

FUN FACT

Suzuki's slogan is "Way of Life!" because it wants to bring excitement to people's lives.

SUZUKI MOTOR COMPANY

Suzuki doesn't make only dirt bikes. It makes ATVs and street motorcycles. It also makes boat motors and cars. It doesn't sell cars in the United States anymore. But Suzuki was the third-best-selling car brand in Japan in 2018.

CHAPTER 3

Suzuki Selection

Kara takes a deep breath. It's race day. She climbs onto her bike. It's a Suzuki RM-Z250. She's never had a Suzuki before. But her brother convinced her to try one. Now she loves it. She kicks down the **kick-starter**. The engine roars to life. She loves the feeling of a kick-starter. It's fun to start the engine this way. Kara bounces her front wheel against the starting gate. Then the gate drops. She twists the **throttle** toward her. This year's model has a great throttle response. It's better than old models. Kara speeds ahead!

She turns around the first corner. The front tire grips the ground. Suzuki bikes are known for handling corners well. The RM-Z250 lives up to expectations. Its light frame helps her steer. This track has lots of tight twists and turns. It's like her bike was made to ride this course.

FUN FACT

Suzuki was the first dirt bike maker to win an FIM Motocross World Championship in all three engine classes.

The 2019 RM-Z250 has more power than previous models.

A jump is coming up. Kara braces herself. She flies over it. She lands hard. But the suspension absorbs the impact. She zooms ahead. She hears her family cheering in the stands. The bike came with very stiff suspension. But it has a coil spring fork. That style is easy to adjust. She loosened it a little when she got it. Now it's just right for her. She races forward along the track. She smiles as she approaches another jump. With the RM-Z250, jumps are her specialty.

BIKE MODEL	RM-Z250	RM-Z450	RMX450Z
SUITABLE FOR	Motocross	Motocross	Off-road/Trail Riding
ENGINE SIZE	250cc	450cc	450cc
TYPE OF START	Kick-starter	Kick-starter	Electric with backup kick-starter
WEIGHT	247 pounds (112 kg)	233 pounds (106 kg)	272 pounds (123.5 kg)
BASE PRICE	$7,899	$8,949	$8,999

COMPARE AND CONTRAST

SUZUKI DIRT BIKES

RM-Z250

RM-Z450

RMX450Z

The RMX450Z is based on the RM-Z450, but redesigned for off-road riding.

Kara's brother James likes watching her race. But he doesn't compete. He'd rather be out in the woods. He zips between trees on his RMX450Z. The bike is built for off-road riding. It's great for cross-country races. But James prefers riding for fun.

James climbs onto the bike. He gets comfortable. He pushes the electric start button. The bike has a kick-starter for backup. But the electric start is easier.

The RMX450Z has lots of trail-riding features. A plate under the engine protects it from scrapes and rocks. The suspension can be adjusted for any trail. The bike also has a headlight. Maybe James will race this bike one day. He knows it would be a champion. But he's happy just exploring. The RMX450Z makes it easy.

CHAPTER 4

Turning Yellow to Gold

Chad Reed is proud to be a Suzuki racer. He started his career on Suzuki when he was around ten years old. He won his first pro championship on a Suzuki. Now he's a supercross star. In 2004, he was the first Australian to win an AMA Supercross race. He's won forty-four supercross main events. Only three other racers have won more than he has. He's raced for other brands before. But he came back to Suzuki in 2018.

Reed straddles his RM-Z450. Tonight, he's competing in the first-ever Supercross FIM Oceania Championship. It's November 2018. Reed wants to do well. Oceania is his home turf.

He speeds through the muddy track. He zooms to the lead. The other racers struggle behind him. But he sails over jumps. He pulls farther and farther ahead. He does a trick over a jump. He turns the bike to the side. Then he sticks one leg straight out behind him. It looks cool. He crosses the finish line. Reed wins! He's the first FIM Oceania Supercross champion. He's excited!

FUN FACT
Reed's racing number is 22.

Chad Reed races supercross inside stadiums.

Vicki Golden made X Games history when she won a bronze medal in Moto X Best Whip in 2013. She was the only female competitor.

FUN FACT
Vicki Golden now competes in freestyle motocross. She does high-flying tricks on dirt bikes.

Vicki Golden knows motocross isn't just for boys. She won X Games Women's Moto X Racing gold three years in a row. She didn't race only with other women. In 2015, she was the first woman to compete in Monster Energy Supercross. She fought against men all season. She wanted to qualify for a supercross night show. The night shows are the main events. They're shown on TV. Viewers would see that girls can do anything boys can do.

Golden struggled all season. She was very sick. She didn't qualify for a main event for months. Finally, she went to the last round of the season. She raced in Las Vegas. Her hair flew behind her from under her helmet. She gripped the handles of her RM-Z250F. She raced hard. It paid off. She qualified! She competed in the main event that night.

Suzuki bikes have come a long way from the Power Free. The company continues to improve its models. And Suzuki riders break down barriers. Their yellow bikes streak around tracks. For Suzuki racers, the brand really is a way of life.

Suzuki continues to innovate, making bikes for everyone.

FUN FACT
Suzuki's signature color is yellow.

BEYOND THE BOOK

After reading the book, it's time to think about what you learned. Try the following exercises to jumpstart your ideas.

THINK

THAT'S NEWS TO ME. Chad Reed won the first-ever Supercross FIM Oceania Championship. How might news sources be able to fill in more detail on this event? What new information could you find in news articles? Where could you go to find those news sources?

CREATE

PRIMARY SOURCES. Primary sources provide original, firsthand accounts of events. Some examples of primary sources could be videos, interviews, or photographs. Make a list of different primary sources you might be able to find on Suzuki dirt bikes. What new information might you learn from these sources?

SHARE

SUM IT UP. Write one paragraph summarizing the important points from this book. Make sure it's in your own words. Don't just copy what is in the text. Then share your summary with a classmate. Does your classmate have any comments about the summary? Do they have additional questions about Suzuki dirt bikes?

GROW

REAL-LIFE RESEARCH. What places could you visit to learn more about Suzuki dirt bikes? What other things could you learn while you were there?

RESEARCH NINJA

Visit *www.ninjaresearcher.com/0943* to learn how to take your research skills and book report writing to the next level!

RESEARCH

DIGITAL LITERACY TOOLS

SEARCH LIKE A PRO
Learn about how to use search engines to find useful websites.

FACT OR FAKE?
Discover how you can tell a trusted website from an untrustworthy resource.

TEXT DETECTIVE
Explore how to zero in on the information you need most.

SHOW YOUR WORK
Research responsibly—learn how to cite sources.

WRITE

GET TO THE POINT
Learn how to express your main ideas.

PLAN OF ATTACK
Learn prewriting exercises and create an outline.

DOWNLOADABLE REPORT FORMS

Further Resources

BOOKS

Adamson, Thomas K. *Motocross Racing*. Bellwether Media, 2016.

Scheff, Matt. *Dirt Bikes*. Abdo Publishing, 2015.

Shaffer, Lindsay. *Dirt Bikes*. Bellwether Media, 2019.

WEBSITES

FACTSURFER

Factsurfer.com gives you a safe, fun way to find more information.

1. Go to www.factsurfer.com.
2. Enter "Suzuki Dirt Bikes" into the search box and click .
3. Select your book cover to see a list of related websites.

Glossary

amateurs: Amateurs are athletes who aren't paid to compete. Suzuki helps amateurs who are working to be professionals.

fork: The fork of a bike is the piece that connects the handlebars to the front wheel. Some Suzuki bikes have a gold-painted fork.

holeshot: In motocross, a racer gets the holeshot by making it to the first corner before the other racers. Mai hoped that training at Camp Carmichael would help her to get the holeshot.

kick-starter: A kick-starter is a lever on a dirt bike's engine that riders kick down in order to start the bike. Kara pushed the kick-starter down and the engine turned on.

looms: Looms are devices used for weaving fabric. Suzuki's company started out making and selling looms.

motocross: Motocross is a type of dirt bike race that takes place on an outdoor dirt track. Mai sped around the motocross track and flew over hills and jumps.

supercross: Supercross is a type of motocross that takes place in a stadium or arena on a man-made dirt course. Chad Reed is a two-time supercross champion.

suspension: A vehicle's suspension is the system that supports its body and absorbs shock from bumps and other impact. The RM-Z250 comes with a very stiff suspension.

throttle: The throttle of a vehicle controls the flow of fuel to the engine. A dirt bike's throttle is controlled by a part on the right handlebar.

Index

PHOTO CREDITS

The images in this book are reproduced through the courtesy of: smileimage9/Shutterstock Images, front cover, p. 9; Suzuki Press, pp. 3, 8, 17, 19 (top), 19 (middle), 19 (bottom), 20, 20–21, 26–27, 30; Corr/iStockphoto, p. 4; Sonrak/Shutterstock Images, pp. 4–5; Reed Saxon/AP Images, p. 6; yevgeniy11/Shutterstock Images, p. 7; Violetta Derkach/Shutterstock Images, pp. 10–11; Jean-Yves Ruszniewski/TempSport/Corbis/VCG/Corbis Sport/Getty Images, pp. 12–13; oneinchpunch/Shutterstock Images, p. 14; Svetlana Arapova/Shutterstock Images, p. 15; Red Line Editorial, pp. 18–19; Charles Mitchell/Icon Sportswire, pp. 22–23; Anthony Anex/Keystone/AP Images, pp. 24–25.

ABOUT THE AUTHOR

R. L. Van is a writer and editor from Minnesota. She loves books, animals, and crossword puzzles.